Basinet
Helmet

Knight

Joan's
Coat of
Arms

Hand-cannon

Joan
in her
armour

A Ladybird
History Book
Series 561

*Joan of Arc was a deeply religious country
girl, with the practical common sense of
one who had worked on a farm since
childhood. The English soldiers believed
she was a witch and were afraid of her: the
French soldiers believed she was a saint
and followed her: the French courtiers and
bishops were jealous of her and betrayed
her. Who shall say which was right: all
we know is that she saved France.*

JOAN OF ARC

by L. DU GARDE PEACH, M.A., Ph.D., D.Litt.

with illustrations
by JOHN KENNEY

Ladybird Books Ltd Loughborough

JOAN OF ARC

In another book in this series you may read the story of King Henry V and of the English victory over the French in 1415 at the battle of Agincourt. This, and other victories gained by Henry, made England master of a large part of France. Henry himself was married to the daughter of the French King, and was named as the heir to the French throne.

However, Henry died at the age of 35, and his son had none of his father's warlike qualities. Although the English forces were able to hold northern France for a time, almost everything that Henry V had won was lost within thirty years.

This was due to a peasant girl from the little village of Domrémy in Lorraine. Her name was Joan, re-membered for ever in history as Joan of Arc.

It is very difficult for us to imagine what France was like in those days. No-one was safe. Soldiers of either side, or even of none, roamed the desolate countryside, burning farms and villages, among them the village of Domrémy where Joan lived. Even the cattle learnt to know the meaning of the sound of the warning bell, and ran to shelter of their own accord when it was rung.

0 7214 0282 8

As a child Joan was not very different from other children. She played the games which all children play, and roamed the lovely woods and fields which still today surround the village of Domrémy. She worked on her father's farm, tending the cattle, and in the winter evenings learnt to spin and sew.

Joan was a quiet, religious girl, and loved to go to church with her parents. Sometimes, when the other children were playing and laughing on the village green, she would sit all alone in the village church. No doubt the other children thought this was unusual, but Joan was a strong, healthy girl and did as she pleased.

Thirty years afterwards, the people of the village who had known her were asked what sort of girl she was. Even though it was so long ago, we have a record of what they said. It was in French of course, but these were their words:

"Joan was such that all the people of Domrémy were fond of her. She was modest, simple, and devout; went gladly to church and to sacred places; worked, served, hoed in the fields, and did what was needful about the house."

The simple people of Domrémy would have been very surprised if they had known that before she was eighteen, this quiet little girl was to become the most famous woman ever to be born in France.

Joan loved listening to the church bells. One day as the sound of them came to her in the quiet of her father's garden, she seemed to hear voices speaking to her in the notes of the bells. She was only thirteen, and at first she was, as she said afterwards, "in great fear."

The voices were friendly and kind. They told her always to be a good girl, and to go often to church. As Joan had no wish to be anything else, and went willingly to church, there was nothing very wonderful in this.

But soon Joan began to see strange visions as she listened to the voices. At first they were as though seen through a mist, but later Joan said, "I saw them with my bodily eyes as clearly as I see you, and when they disappeared I used to weep and be very unhappy." Joan grew to love her voices so much that she used to give little presents to the bell-ringer.

By the time Joan was sixteen the visions had assumed for her the figures of St. Michael and the two patron saints of Lorraine, St. Catherine and St. Margaret.

They had a new message for the peasant girl of Domrémy. They told her that she was to be the saviour of her country by driving the hated English into the sea. She was to lead the armies of France to victory, and to crown a young King, Charles VII, at Rheims.

French soldiers were everywhere being defeated by the English, and the French people were utterly disheartened, wretched, and without hope. Everywhere crops were ungathered and rotting in the fields, and all trade was at a standstill.

It seemed impossible that a simple, village girl could do anything against the thousands of rough English soldiers who were terrorising the countryside, and at first Joan refused to believe what her voices told her. There was however an old prophesy to the effect that a maid from the Lorraine border would one day save France. It is very probable that Joan had heard of this prophesy and, as she listened to the bells, she began to see herself as the chosen maid.

The town of Orléans was being besieged by the English with an army of 10,000 men. If they captured it, the way would be open to them for the conquest of the whole of the southern half of France.

Joan's voices told her to go to Orléans and relieve the city by driving the English away.

At first, she said, she was puzzled and unhappy. In her distress of mind she went to her father, who was a leading man in the village of Domrémy. Although she was only sixteen, Joan had the commonsense of a girl brought up in the country, but to her father she was still a child. He laughed at her and no doubt told her not to be silly.

Joan went back to minding the cattle and working in the fields, but her voices continued to urge her to action. Again she went to her father. This time he was angry. He said that rather than let her do anything so foolish, he would drown her with his own hands. Of course he would never have done anything of the sort, but he believed that what his daughter wanted to do was both stupid and wicked.

Joan was a very religious girl, and she firmly believed that God was speaking to her through her voices. She dared not disobey them.

The walled town of Vaucouleurs, about ten or twelve miles from Domrémy, was commanded by a French nobleman named Robert Baudricourt. Joan determined to go to him and to ask for his help. She knew that her father would never permit this, so she went first to a village near Vaucouleurs to stay with a relation of her mother.

To him she told what her voices had ordered her to do. He was doubtful, but Joan was determined and insistent. Finally he agreed to take her to see de Baudricourt.

Robert de Baudricourt refused to have anything to do with her. We can imagine the astonishment of this French nobleman when a simple peasant girl, in a much worn, red woollen dress, told him that she was sent by Heaven to save France. "Box her ears and send her home," he told Laxart. But Joan was not to be put off. The French soldiers were everywhere being defeated by the English. Something had to be done, and de Baudricourt at last began to wonder whether there might be something in what Joan said.

It was a superstitious age. People still believed in witches and direct signs from Heaven. Robert de Baudricourt thought that if the French soldiers believed Joan was really sent by Heaven to lead them, it might put some heart into them.

The French had just lost a battle called the Battle of the Herrings because they had failed to stop a convoy with loads of herrings getting to the English camp outside Orléans. The French garrison inside the city was offering to surrender, forced by famine. Joan seemed to de Baudricourt to be the last hope.

Charles VII was at Chinon, three hundred miles away from Vaucouleurs. To get there, Joan would have to ride right across France, through country held by the English and the soldiers of Burgundy, who were fighting on the English side against France. It would be a very dangerous journey.

Joan set out on horseback, accompanied by two young French noblemen. Her voices had told her to dress as a man, so she cut her hair short and put on a dark doublet and hose. Robert de Baudricourt gave her an old sword, saying, "Go, and let come what may." It was not a very encouraging send-off.

It was winter, and to avoid the English soldiers the party had to travel by small by-roads, which were often mere tracks. There were also two wide rivers to cross, and they knew the bridges would be watched and guarded.

The journey took eleven days. Often they had to spend the night in the open, because it was too dangerous to seek shelter. Very wet and weary they arrived at the little town of Chinon, only to find that it was not easy to enter into the presence of the King.

Chinon has changed very little since Joan of Arc dismounted from her horse to climb up to the castle. The old gabled houses and steep, crooked streets are as Joan knew them more than five hundred years ago.

The castle, now a ruin, stands on a high cliff above the river Vienne, a tributary of the Loire. It was in this castle that an English king, Richard Coeur de Lion, about whom you may read in another book in this series, had his court two hundred years earlier. High up on the wall of a room in the ruins is an inscribed stone, telling how, in this room, Joan of Arc first met the Dauphin, Charles VII.

Charles was weak in body and mind, and completely at the mercy of his counsellors. At first they refused to allow him to receive Joan, but the people had heard of her mission and it might have been dangerous to deny her.

None of them believed her story of her voices, and in order to discredit her, they disguised Charles as one of the courtiers and caused another young man to sit on the throne. This was to be the test of whether Joan's voices were true or not. If they were, they argued, she would not be deceived.

Joan, travel stained and still dressed in her doublet and hose, was brought into the midst of the brilliant court. She looked round, wondering at the fine ladies in their rich dresses. The courtiers laughed. This, they thought, was the end of her silly story.

It is told in the writings of those who were present, that the peasant girl smiled and shook her head at the young man on the throne. Turning away, she went straight to the disguised Charles, and going on her knees, said, "I am God's messenger to tell you that you are to be the true King of France."

Charles was convinced that Joan had indeed been sent to restore his kingdom, but the counsellors still doubted. They insisted that she be further examined by a body of learned men and high priests of the Church.

Joan probably wondered what all the fuss was about. She answered all their questions with the straightforward honesty of a simple peasant girl. "I cannot read or write," she said, "but I know that my voices have commanded me to raise the siege of Orléans and crown the King at Rheims."

Joan was a country girl in surroundings which might well have embarrassed or frightened her. She was neither embarrassed nor frightened. When one of her examiners, who had a very rough, uncouth way of speaking, tried to catch her out by asking in what accent her voices spoke to her, she smiled and said, "Better than thine."

Her simple faith convinced the priests: it did not convince the counsellors who surrounded Charles. But things were going from bad to worse for France and they were ready to try anything. Although in their opinion Joan was only a deluded peasant girl, they thought the soldiers might regard her as a sort of mascot. They agreed to send her to Orléans.

In order to impress the French soldiers, Joan was given a suit of armour, with a surcoat of white and scarlet. In front of her was carried a banner with a picture of Christ emblazoned on it. She is said to have looked "a thing wholly Divine."

Many stories and legends are told about those who, like Joan of Arc, become famous in the history of a country. Some of them may be true, some not.

One of the stories told of Joan of Arc is about the horse which she was given to ride, a more spirited steed than the one she had ridden from Vaucouleurs. It plunged and reared up and would not allow her to mount. "Lead it to the cross," she said. The horse was taken to the cross in the market place where it stood quietly.

There is also the legend of the sword of Martel, a French hero who six centuries before had saved France from the Moslems. Joan asked for it to be brought from where it had been hidden for centuries, behind the altar in a church at Fierbois. No-one knew anything about it, but when they dug behind the altar, it was found and brought to Joan.

So Joan was sent with a suitable escort to Blois, half way between Chinon and Orléans. Here she was given command of 6,000 men. Charles' counsellors probably hoped that when she found herself, a peasant girl of seventeen, in command of an army, she would lose her nerve and run away back to Domrémy.

Joan was made of sterner stuff. The soldiers were no doubt surprised when they saw her, and learnt that they were to obey her orders. They were even more surprised when she insisted that they should first all go to church.

One of the commanders was a man from Gascony named la Hire. He was a good commander and a brave man, but like so many soldiers, he used a lot of bad language. Joan told him that this must cease, and he was so surprised that he obeyed.

The English were scornful. They regarded Joan as a witch who had put a spell on the French King. At the same time they were uncomfortable. In the year 1428 everyone believed that witches had the power to do harm. In the play Henry VI, part I, Shakespeare takes the English view of Joan, describing her as the fiend of France.

Before setting out from Blois, Joan, who could neither read nor write, dictated a letter to the King of England and his generals, saying that she had been sent by God to restore France to the rightful king, and demanding that they deliver up all the French towns which they had captured.

Receiving no reply, Joan rode at the head of the army to Orléans, to find that the English had built a series of strongpoints, called 'bastilles', round the town. Her intention was to evade the English and to enter the town with her soldiers. This would add 6,000 men to the garrison, and they would be strong enough to attack the English.

When she arrived at Orléans, Joan found that the French commanders had deceived her. They were angry because she had been put in command over them. They wanted her to fail, and had led her to the south side of the river Loire. Orléans was on the north side, and a contrary wind made it impossible to cross the broad stream.

Then suddenly the wind changed. This made the English even more certain that Joan was a witch, and that she had used witchcraft to make the wind blow in her favour.

Joan had brought much-needed food and arms for the beleaguered garrison. As there were not enough boats to carry all the soldiers over the river, Joan sent most of them to cross by a bridge, lower down. She herself crossed by boat, and was greeted by cheering crowds. Her story had gone before her, and the people were now certain that Heaven was on her side.

When the English soldiers heard the church bells ringing and the cheers of the people, they were struck with superstitious fear. When next morning the French soldiers, having crossed the river, marched into the town, the English were too frightened of 'the witch' to stop them.

In those days armies faced one another at close range. Joan hated the idea of anyone being killed, and with the river between them, she called to the English commander to raise the siege and march away. She received mocking replies and returned sadly to her quarters.

Although she disliked the thought of fighting, Joan was herself as brave as any of her soldiers. She led them again and again, urging them on and waving her sword, though there is no record that she ever used it. She did not need to.

In order to drive the English away, it was necessary to capture the strongpoints with which they had surrounded Orléans. Whilst Joan was resting, the French commanders marched out to attack one of them, named the Augustines. Awakened by the sound of the fighting, Joan rapidly put on her armour and went towards the noise of the battle.

The English were getting the best of it, and the French were on the point of retreating when Joan appeared in their midst. Her shining armour and the banner which she carried, but even more her presence, rallied the French forces. Shouting "The Maid! The Maid!" they turned on the English who, terrified of witchcraft, fled headlong.

Two days later Joan led her now devoted soldiers against another strongpoint, the Tourelles. In the forefront of the attack, Joan herself placed the first ladder against the wall of the fort. As she climbed it, she was wounded by an arrow in the shoulder.

Joan was carried to the rear to have her wound dressed. Seeing her go, weak with the pain of the wound, the French lost heart. Dunois, the commander, was about to order the retreat when Joan reappeared, and the strongpoint was captured.

The siege of Orléans was over. Disheartened, and believing as they did that it was useless to try to fight against witchcraft, the English marched away. There was general rejoicing in the city. The churches were full of people, led by Joan herself, giving thanks to God for the victory.

Everyone in France, except some of the counsellors and priests who were jealous of her, believed that Joan had been sent miraculously to save the country. The soldiers were ready to follow her anywhere. What was more important, the English soldiers only fought half-heartedly, and often ran away when they knew that 'the witch' was leading the French army.

The relief of Orléans by Joan of Arc has never been forgotten by the people who live in the city. A statue of her has been erected to her memory, and every year the anniversary of the raising of the siege is celebrated.

Especially remembered is the taking of the strong-point, the Tourelles, the capture of which ensured victory for the French. A simple cross was set up on the left bank of the river Loire, to mark the spot where the fort had stood.

The relief of Orléans was only the beginning. There were still thousands of English soldiers in France, occupying French towns, burning French villages and spreading destruction everywhere. These English had to be met and defeated before Joan could finish the task commanded by her voices and crown Charles at Rheims.

The French soldiers, who previously had been afraid of the English, now wanted to find and to fight them. They were given new courage by the belief that with Joan to lead them, victory was certain.

Joan's voices had told her that she had only one year in which to save France. There was no time to be lost. From Orléans she marched to where she knew the English had occupied other and smaller towns near Orléans.

The first of these was Jargeau, only ten miles away. The garrison was commanded by an English nobleman, the Earl of Suffolk, but his soldiers had not recovered from their defeat at Orléans. When they saw Joan on her white horse leading the attack, they were almost paralysed with fear. The French charged through the town, with Joan in the thick of the fighting. The town was captured, and the Earl of Suffolk taken prisoner.

Joan allowed her soldiers no rest. She probably thought that the best thing to do was to strike at the English before they had time to recover. Marching quickly to another small town, Beaugency, twenty-five miles away, she captured it before moving on to her most famous victory at Patay, twenty miles to the north.

If you look up these places on the map, you will see that they form a triangle, with Orléans in the middle. It was necessary for Joan to capture them to break out of the triangle.

By now the English were utterly demoralised by superstitious terror. When Joan and her soldiers suddenly appeared out of the mist on a June morning, the battle was half won.

At the battle of Agincourt, fourteen years earlier, the English archers had protected themselves by driving a row of sharp pointed stakes into the ground across the front of their line. From behind these they shot their deadly arrows at the French knights. Joan attacked them at Patay before they could fix their stakes. Charging down on them, the French slew more than a third of their number. The rest fled or surrendered, and their commander, Lord Talbot, was captured, together with many English knights.

It was a long march to Rheims, but the English were so disheartened, and so afraid of witchcraft, that they retreated to Paris and offered no interference. Joan marched with her victorious French soldiers by way of Troyes, a distance of more than 200 miles.

The coronation of Charles in the great cathedral at Rheims was performed with great splendour. The high priests of the Church in their vestments, the nobles in brilliant costumes, and the ladies in wonderful dresses, all made a glowing picture in the light streaming through the stained glass windows. But the figure which took all eyes was that of Joan the Maid.

In her shining armour, holding the banner which had led France to victory, she stood by the King as he was solemnly crowned. It was a wonderful moment for the peasant girl from Domremy, a girl only seventeen years old.

With the coronation of the King, Joan felt that the mission commanded by her voices was finished. She wished to return to her simple life in Lorraine. "The pleasure of God is done," she said. "Would that I might go and keep sheep once more with my brothers and sisters." But it was not to be.

Although the commanders of the French army were all jealous of Joan, they knew that it was she who was responsible for the victories which had been won. The French soldiers followed her as they would follow no one else.

Before Joan appeared, a mere handful of English men-at-arms would cause hundreds of French soldiers to run from the field. Now it was the other way about. Joan was extremely brave. Her example made her soldiers fight as they had never fought before. The stories of her supernatural powers inspired the French, but struck terror into the hearts of the superstitious English.

Joan dedicated her sword and armour to the Virgin Mary in the church of St. Denis in Rheims. Her voices had ceased to speak to her of victories to be won. Again and again she asked to go back to Domrémy: always she was refused.

Joan was very unhappy. She was the heroine of France; all the common people loved her; everywhere she went people knelt for her blessing, and rough soldiers cheered her with tears in their eyes. Only at the court of Charles VII, who owed his crown to her, did she find jealousy and contempt.

Paris was still held by the English. The French commanders knew that without Joan to lead and inspire the soldiers, they had little chance of taking it. Against her will they persuaded her again to take the field.

It was with a heavy heart that she put on her armour. She remembered the warning that she had only a year in which to complete her task. The year had now run out.

The attack on Paris failed. The French commanders allowed their jealousy of Joan to triumph over their patriotism. Although the French soldiers fought bravely, there were not enough of them, and the English had received reinforcements.

Joan led her army with the courage and indifference to danger of her earlier battles. As always, she was where the fighting was most fierce. At the attack on the gate St. Honoré, the French soldiers began to draw back. Joan went forward alone, calling on them to follow her, but as they did so, she was again wounded. As the battle raged round her, Joan lay in a ditch, refusing to leave until the gate was captured. But seeing her fall, the soldiers lost heart. They retreated, carrying Joan with them, too weak to resist.

The French commanders were secretly glad that Joan had been repulsed, and Charles, who was weak and a coward, retired to Bourges.

Joan again asked to be allowed to return to Domrémy, but again permission was refused by the selfish King. Instead, Joan was given a title and promised an income which was never paid. In addition, the village of Domrémy was exempted from the payment of taxes. Joan was happy to think that what she had done had benefited her native village, but she would far rather have returned to it.

The Duke of Burgundy had been fighting on the side of the English. Now he agreed to a truce, which lasted until the spring of the following year, 1430.

It was in 1428 that Joan relieved Orléans. The year promised by her voices had long been exceeded, and at a successful battle at Melun, a few miles south-east of Paris, her voices again spoke to her. "As I was on the ramparts at Melun" she said, "St. Catherine and St. Margaret warned me that I would be captured before Midsummer Day. I prayed that when I was taken I might die in that hour without the wretchedness of long captivity."

It was in May, 1430, that the warning given to Joan of Arc by her voices came true.

The town of Compiègne was being besieged by the soldiers of the Duke of Burgundy. Although Charles was still sulking at Bourges, Joan went with a detachment of French soldiers to relieve Compiègne. She led the attack with her usual bravery and fought her way into the town. It seemed as though the raising of the siege of Orléans was to be repeated at Compiègne.

At Orléans Joan had made one sortie after another, capturing the strongpoints round the town. Her attacks had been successful at Orléans and she repeated them at Compiègne. Several sorties were made, and the Burgundians were being driven back when they suddenly counter-attacked. As the French withdrew, Joan was in a place of danger in the rear of the retreat. Almost deserted by the French soldiers, whose only desire was to get back into the town, Joan was surrounded and pulled off her horse.

Joan was now a prisoner in the hands of the Duke of Burgundy. Although he knew that he was condemning her to certain death, this despicable French nobleman sold her to the English for 10,000 livres.

To his everlasting disgrace, the cowardly King of France did nothing to help the peasant girl who had saved France and won for him his royal crown. The one thing the English wanted was to be revenged upon her for the humiliation she had brought on them. They were only too ready to conspire with the crafty and deceitful Bishop of Beauvais to buy her from the Burgundians.

Joan knew what her fate would be if she fell into the hands of the English. In an attempt to avoid it, she jumped from a window sixty feet above ground and was badly hurt. It made no difference. She was handed over to her bitterest enemies and kept in chains in a damp, dark cell for many weeks.

After a long and hideously unfair trial, presided over by the dastardly Bishop who had been bribed to sell her to the English, Joan was condemned for witchcraft and burnt in the market place at Rouen. The Church, which condemned her to martyrdom in 1430, welcomed her as a saint in 1919.

The famous statue pictured opposite was carved by Emmanuel Frémiet and shows Joan in her armour praying for heavenly guidance before a battle.

Crossbow-men

Longbowman

Salade Helmet

Spearman

A Bombard